Can Science Solve?

The Mystery
of
Stone Circles

Paul Mason

Heinemann
LIBRARY

www.heinemann.co.uk/library
Visit our website to find out more information about **Heinemann Library** books.

To order:
☎ Phone 44 (0) 1865 888066
🖹 Send a fax to 44 (0) 1865 314091
 Visit the Heinemann Bookshop at www.heinemann.co.uk/library to browse our
   catalogue and order online.

First published in Great Britain by Heinemann Library,
Halley Court, Jordan Hill, Oxford OX2 8EJ,
a division of Reed Educational and Professional Publishing Ltd.
Heinemann is a registered trademark of Reed Educational & Professional Publishing
Limited.

OXFORD MELBOURNE AUCKLAND
JOHANNESBURG BLANTYRE GABORONE
IBADAN PORTSMOUTH NH (USA) CHICAGO

Designed by AMR
Illustrations by Art Construction
Origination by Ambassador Litho Ltd.
Printed in Hong Kong/China

ISBN 0 431 01625 9
06 05 04 03 02
10 9 8 7 6 5 4 3 2 1

British Library Cataloguing in Publication Data

Mason, Paul
  Can science solve the mystery of stone circles?
  1.Stone circles – Juvenile literature
  I.Title II.Stone circles
  930.1'4

Acknowledgements
The Publishers would like to thank the following for permission to reproduce
photographs: Collections/Fay Godwin: p16; Fortean Picture Library: pp7, 8, 10, 25, 27,
29; Imagebank: p18; Mary Evans Picture Library: pp14, 22; Rob Pilgrim: p11; Science
Photo Library: pp5, 12, 13, 15, 17, 24; The British Museum: p19.

Cover photograph reproduced with permission of Robert Harding Picture Library.

Every effort has been made to contact copyright holders of any material reproduced in
this book. Any omissions will be rectified in subsequent printings if notice is given to
the Publisher.

Any words appearing in the text in bold, **like this**, are explained in the Glossary.

Contents

It's a mysterious world

For tens of thousands of years humans have found their surroundings strange and mysterious. Why does the sun sometimes disappear from the sky, blanked out by the moon? What causes the nights to get longer and the weather to get colder in winter? Why is the sky lit up by strange forked lightning during terrible storms? Science has now found the answers to these questions.

Other puzzles come from the past. One of the greatest mysteries surrounds the ancient stone circles that are scattered around France, England, Scotland and Ireland. There have been many theories about these circles, when they were built and what they were used for. But it was only after the Second World War that scientists began to study the stone circles in earnest, trying to discover the answers to some of these questions. But have they succeeded?

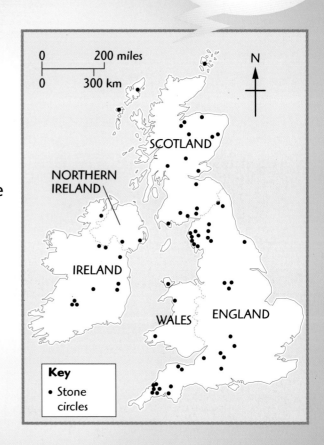

The stone circles of the British Isles

Stone circle briefing

Some circles are simple – a few large stones arranged in a circle. Others are complicated and must have taken many generations to build. A few circles feature giant stones. Ancient people had only simple tools. How were stones weighing many tonnes lifted without modern machinery?

The secret language of the stones

cairn   *a mound of stones used as a marker of some kind. Cairns are often conical in shape.*

dolmen   *an ancient tomb with a large, flat stone laid on top of upright ones.*

henge   *a circular earth bank, often found around the outer edge of a stone circle.*

menhir   *a single **standing stone**.*

The circles have stood for thousands of years, and for almost all that time they have been a mystery to both visitors and people living nearby. At first, people simply wondered how they had been built, and why. But as we have discovered more about the stone circles, their mysteries have deepened still further.

The circles seem to use mathematical techniques that scientists believed had not been discovered until long after the circles were built. Some circles were built from giant stones that came from hundreds of kilometres away – no one could work out how they had been moved. Circles hundreds of kilometres apart used the same unit of measurement in their layout. Most mysterious of all, some of these ancient sites seemed to **align** with one another over huge distances.

With so many puzzles to solve, scientists had a real challenge

Stonehenge

High on the open landscape of Salisbury Plain in England stands the most famous, most studied and most mysterious stone circle of all: Stonehenge. Many people first see Stonehenge from a distance, as they drive towards it along the road from Salisbury. Seen this way, the stones appear quite small, but up close their giant size becomes clear. The largest of them stands 6.7 metres high, another 2.4 metres of the stone is buried below ground. Standing on top, you could easily see into the second storey windows of a house.

The Avenue

The way into Stonehenge is along a pathway known as the Avenue, which leads between two banks. At the entrance to the circle is a large, red-stained stone, lying on its side. People once thought that this red colour was a result of the stone being used for human **sacrifices**, and it is still called the Slaughter Stone. In fact, scientists have now worked out that the red colour comes from rainwater reacting with the iron in the stone over thousands of years.

Stonehenge consists of several circles, each inside another. At the outside edge of the site are the Aubrey Holes (named after John Aubrey, the man who discovered them in the 1600s). The washed, burnt bones of human beings were found in the bottom of some of these 56 holes.

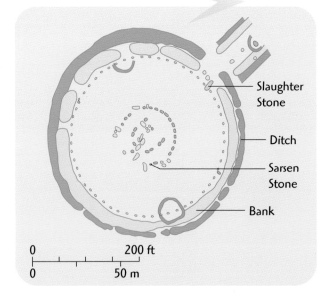

The layout of Stonehenge seen from above.

Slaughter Stone

Ditch

Sarsen Stone

Bank

0   200 ft

0   50 m

The sarsen stones

The most dramatic part of Stonehenge is the central circle of giant **sarsen** stones. Some have now fallen or have been pulled over, but originally they were arranged as a giant circle of upright stones, crowned with another set of huge sarsens – called **lintel** stones – on top. Each group of three stones arranged in this way is called a **trilithon**. Some of the trilithons are still standing. It is hard to imagine how they could possibly have been erected without the help of some sort of crane. You can read how scientists worked out the answer to this riddle on page 20.

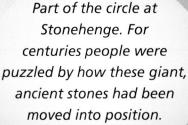

Part of the circle at Stonehenge. For centuries people were puzzled by how these giant, ancient stones had been moved into position.

Another of the mysteries of Stonehenge is how the stones came to be there. Some of them come from a site in Wales that is over 300 kilometres away. How could the ancient people who built Stonehenge have moved the stones such a huge distance?

Strange Stonehenge

One of the earliest mentions of Stonehenge was made by the historian Geoffrey of Monmouth. In AD 1135, he described several rival theories about how Stonehenge had been built. Some people claimed it had first been brought to Ireland from Africa by a tribe of giants, then flown across the sea by the wizard Merlin. Other people said that the stones had been stolen from an Irish woman by the Devil, then put on Salisbury Plain by Merlin for the King of the Britons, Ambrosius Aurelianus.

Carnac

Carnac is a small town on the southern coast of Brittany in France. It lies in a sheltered spot, good for agriculture and fishing. The area would have been an excellent place for ancient people to live, and indeed many thousands of them made it their home. We know this from the evidence they left behind, in the form of **standing stones**. Carnac is surrounded by an amazing number of ancient stones. Some are single stones called **menhirs**, but most of the stones have been laid out in a mysterious pattern.

Many of Carnac's stones are laid out in mysterious rows known as alignments.

Alignments

Spread across the landscape are lines of standing stones, called **alignments**. Without actually visiting the area around Carnac, it is almost impossible to imagine the impact of these alignments when you first see them. There are thousands of stones spread across a vast area, so many that they seem impossible to count. Only later do you start to see that they are not just scattered randomly across the fields. Each stone has been placed deliberately in position, although it is unclear for what purpose.

Stone circles

Stone circles are more unusual in Brittany than in the British Isles, but there are at least four near to Carnac, with others slightly further away. The largest of these is Kerlescan, but one of the most interesting is at Le Ménec. The circle here is actually the shape of an egg, although the original shape is hard to see now as many stones were taken to use in building the nearby village of Le Ménec.

The circle at Le Ménec is so large that it could once have held 1000 people. Leading towards it are eleven aligned avenues of standing stones, looking almost like the snaking ropes that guide queues of people at cinemas or airport check-ins. The straightest of these avenues leads directly to a place where there was originally a wide gap in the circle of stones. It is not hard to imagine this straight avenue as an entranceway that could have brought hundreds of people together inside the circle.

Avebury

Just 30 kilometres north of Stonehenge lies another remarkable stone circle, Avebury. This is the largest stone circle in the world: the outer edge is made up of an **embankment** and ditch that are 1.5 kilometres long. The ditch is now partly filled, but the drop from the top of the embankment to the bottom was originally 17 metres.

Outer and inner rings

Avebury's outer ring was made up of almost 100 stones, though not all of these are still standing. Many were broken up in the 1700s by builders, who used the pieces of stone in their work. Several of the houses they built burned down, adding to a feeling among local people that the stones were **cursed** in some way.

Inside the outer ring are the remains of two smaller stone circles. The largest stone at Avebury, the Swindon Stone, weighs about 60 tonnes. Like all the others, it was somehow moved there from the Marlborough Downs, which are visible on the horizon.

This aerial photo shows the giant size of the Avebury circle. The trench inside the embankment has now partly been filled in, but was once deep enough to hide a two-storey building inside.

Legends about Avebury

Avebury has always been associated with strange goings-on. At the stroke of midnight the Swindon Stone is said to cross the road that runs beside it. Another stone is called the Devil's Chair, it has a seat-shaped dent at its base, worn smooth by millions of bottoms. Legend says that if you run around the Devil's Chair a hundred times in an anticlockwise direction, the Devil himself will appear.

The Devil's Chair at Avebury is surrounded by legend.

The St Michael Alignment

Avebury is also part of a bigger mystery. It is one of fifteen ancient sites that lie along an imaginary straight line that stretches from the far western tip of Cornwall to the eastern tip of East Anglia. This line is called the St Michael **Alignment**. All the sites along the line are thousands of years old, and no one knows how it was possible for the ancient people who built them to line them up.

The unlucky barber

During the 1300s some of the stones at Avebury were buried on the orders of the local priest, who thought they were creations of the Devil. As a worker was hollowing out a chamber underneath one of the stones, it collapsed on top of him and crushed him to death. When his skeleton was removed many years later, he was found to have a pair of scissors and a few silver coins in his pockets, making it likely that he was a barber.

More stone circles

Stonehenge, Avebury and Carnac are among the most famous stone circles, but there are many more circles in England, Ireland, Scotland, France and even Africa.

The Merry Maidens and The Pipers

The Merry Maidens are a circle of nineteen stones situated near the town of Penzance in Cornwall, England. Nearby stand a pair of tall stones, called The Pipers. Local legends tell that these are all that remain of villagers who were turned to stone for dancing on the **sabbath** day. Early Christians thought that it was wrong to do anything on a Sunday except worship God.

These stones make up part of the Merry Maidens stone circle in Cornwall, England.

Drombeg

The stone circle at Drombeg in County Cork, Ireland is known to local people as The Druid's Altar. The **druids** were the leaders of a religion that existed in the British Isles before the Romans came. For many years it was thought that stone circles had been built by the druids. Modern-day druids still worship at Stonehenge and other stone circles, especially on **Midsummer** Day.

Callanish

The stone circle at Callanish is on Stornoway, one of the Outer Hebrides Islands in the Atlantic Ocean, off the west

coast of Scotland. It is a wild, beautiful setting for a stone circle, and Callanish is surrounded by legends. One says that when the giants who lived on the island refused to become Christians, St Kieran turned them to stone.

Kergonan

This is one of the greatest French circles, although it is now badly overgrown with bushes and tangled weeds. Kergonan is also known as the *Cercle de la Mort*, meaning 'the circle of death', and as *Er Anké*. This name comes from a legendary figure called Er Ankeu, a messenger of death, who usually appears as a skeleton wrapped in a white **shroud**. Many stone circles are associated with death in some way, possibly because people thought they had been used as the sites for human **sacrifices**, or perhaps because important people were once buried there.

Wasu

Stone circles also exist in Africa, near the Gambia river. These circles seem to have been built as graveyards for important people. A small stone next to a larger one may show a child buried next to a grown-up, while a V-shaped stone shows that two close relatives died on the same day and were buried next to one another.

Who built the stone circles?

There have been many theories about who built the stone circles. In the Middle Ages, people said that the Romans had built them as great temples. In fact, the Romans were far more skilled as stonemasons than the people who built the stone circles, and would have thought circles like Avebury and Carnac were very roughly made.

Other legends said that Stonehenge was built by King Arthur, or by his friend Merlin the wizard. Sometimes the stone circles were even said to be the work of the Devil, who built them for his followers. For many years people thought the stone circles had been built by the **druids**. Then in 1974, a new theory said that Stonehenge had been built by Egyptian colonists, who found the challenge simple, having built the pyramids not long before!

Druids, shown here collecting mistletoe, were once thought to have built the stone circles.

Dating the stones

The truth about who built the stone circles only began to be discovered when scientists worked out when they had been built. After the Second World War, a technique called **carbon dating** revealed that the circles were far older than anyone had previously realized. The oldest parts of Stonehenge, for example, date back to 3100 BC. The stone circle builders had been at work hundreds of years before the pyramids were built in Egypt. When Stonehenge was begun, the foundation stones for the Greek city of Troy had not yet been laid, the Sumerian army was just about to invent the chariot, and the ancient cultures of Central America were still 1500 years in the future.

Scientists named the time of the stone circle builders the **megalithic** age. 'Megalith' is another word for a large stone, particularly a large **standing stone**.

An array of complicated equipment is used for carbon dating, which was used to work out how old the circles truly were.

Carbon dating

*Carbon dating works by measuring the amount of a particular **element** in an object. For example, a freshly **quarried** piece of rock might have 400 pieces of the element potassium inside it. An old rock of the same type might have only 200 pieces of potassium. If scientists know that rock loses potassium at a rate of one piece every 100 years, they can work out that the rock is 2000 years old.*

The world of the circle builders

What was life like for the people who built the stone circles? Could their lifestyle offer us any clues about what the circles were for?

One of the problems with trying to answer these questions is that the **megalithic** circle builders did not know how to write. Their stories and history were remembered, and retold around the fireplace on cold winter evenings, but never written down. So the only information we have about the megalithic world comes from things its people left behind, in **burial chambers** and abandoned homes.

A wild countryside

North-western Europe was a very different place 5000 years ago. There were very few fields, few cows, no sheep and no horses. The land was almost unaffected by humans: woodland stretched for huge distances, and at night wolves could be heard howling at the moon. Travellers who journeyed into the forests needed to beware of bears, but most would have made their journeys on paths that travelled safely along the open ridges.

Because the circle builders left no written records behind, our main clues to how they lived come from things they left in burial chambers and abandoned houses.

Forests would have been dangerous places for the circle builders, who would have had to dodge wolves like this one, especially if they got caught in the forest at night.

The changing seasons

The circle builders lived much closer to nature than we do now. They were farmers who spent most of their time trying to grow food on poor soil, using very basic tools. Bad weather in summer, when the crops should be ripening, was a catastrophe, so was a long, cold winter unless there was enough food stored to get through it. The changes in the year – from winter to spring, or summer to autumn – would have been very important to these early farmers.

The average megalithic person had a harsh, difficult lifestyle and could only expect to live for about 25 years. There are many things we have yet to discover about the world in which the people of that time lived. But the greatest mystery of all has to be this: when life was so hard, why did they spend so much of their time building enormous stone circles?

Circles through time

No builder who worked on one of the great stone circles would ever have expected to see his work finished. **Carbon dating** *has told us that the circles took thousands of years to complete. Stonehenge, for example, was begun in about 3100 BC, but work on the last stage of its construction was not finished until about 1100 BC. Roughly 80 generations of people had been born and had died in the meantime.*

17

What were the stone circles for?

Over the centuries, there have been lots of theories about what the stone circles were used for. Many now seem likely to be completely wrong, while others contain a grain of truth.

Places of sacrifice

Stones at many sites have been given **gory** names because people thought that the circles had been used for human **sacrifices**. Human remains have been discovered inside stone circles, but no one can be sure whether they were sacrifices, or the bones of important people who were buried there.

People once thought human sacrifices had taken place on this stone, and called it the Slaughter Stone. In fact the reddish colour comes from iron that has been stained rust-coloured.

Devils and demons

Some stone circles have been associated with the Devil and demons for many centuries. Names like 'The Devil's Den', 'The Devil's Brand-Irons' and 'The Devil's **Quoits**' suggest an evil connection. In fact, these names were given to the stones late in their lives, during the early 1300s, by Christian priests. They saw that the circles were associated with older religious beliefs which competed with Christianity. These older beliefs were linked to the passing of the seasons, and involved the worship of a variety of gods and goddesses. Christian priests wanted people to believe in just one god, so they gave the stones names that associated them with the Devil. They encouraged their followers to pull down the **standing stones** and destroy or bury them.

Hidden treasure

Rumours of hidden treasure are sometimes linked to stone circles. None has ever been discovered inside one, but there are a few cases of treasure being found nearby. Close to a stone circle called The Hurlers in Cornwall is a round **barrow**, which for years was said to be the home of a druid whose ghost would sometimes give people a drink from a golden cup. When the barrow was finally opened in 1818, it contained bones and flints just like those found in most other barrows – and a beautiful golden cup.

This gold cup was found in Cornwall in the 19th century.

Temples of the druids

John Aubrey, who discovered the Aubrey Holes at Stonehenge in the 1600s, was one of the first people to take a real interest in stone circles. At this time, people had no knowledge of history before the Romans, who were the first people to leave written records. Roman writings mentioned that when they arrived, Britain was being governed by a group of priests called druids. Aubrey and his followers thought that the stone circles must have been built by the **druids**. In fact, as we now know, the circles were far older than Aubrey suspected.

Hill of the goblins

Bryn-yr-ellyllon – *a round **cairn** whose name is Welsh for 'hill of the goblins' – was said to be haunted by the ghost of a giant. One night in 1810, a husband and wife were crossing a nearby field when they were terrified to see a huge figure 'clothed in a coat of gold which shone like the sun'. Twenty years later, the cairn was excavated: inside was a tall skeleton, hundreds of amber beads and a golden cloak.*

How was Stonehenge built?

One of the great riddles of Stonehenge is how it came to be built. The builders of the circle of giant **sarsen** stones had to move them into place and turn them upright. Then they had to lift the **lintel** stones into position on top. The techniques that they used were a mystery for many years.

Lifting the giant stones

To find out how it might have been done, scientists used **computer models** to test various theories. When they had come up with one that seemed to work, it was time to test their ideas in practice. Hundreds of people using ancient tools came together to discover one of the secrets of Stonehenge. They used only the kind of tools that would have been available to the people who built the circle.

First a hole was dug for a stone to sit in. Giant levers were used to lift the other end up to an angle of about 30 degrees from the ground. Then teams of helpers pulled the stone upright with ropes, so that it stood in the hole. Once two stones were in position, the lintel could be lifted into place, using a wooden framework and a system of pulleys.

Bluestones from Wales

Two types of stone were used to build Stonehenge. The sarsen stones are made of hard sandstone that comes from a site about 30 kilometres north-east of the circle. The smaller stones (which weigh up to 4 tonnes) are made of bluestone from the Preseli Mountains in south-west Wales. Stonehenge was built long before the invention of modern transport –

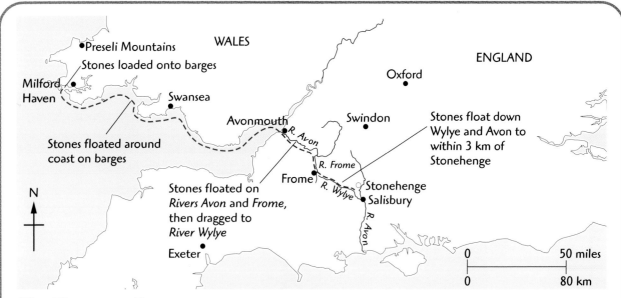

Map labels:
- Preseli Mountains / Stones loaded onto barges
- WALES
- ENGLAND
- Oxford
- Milford Haven
- Swansea
- Avonmouth
- R. Avon
- Swindon
- Stones float down Wylye and Avon to within 3 km of Stonehenge
- Stones floated around coast on barges
- R. Frome
- Frome
- R. Wylye
- Stonehenge
- Salisbury
- R. Avon
- Stones floated on Rivers Avon and Frome, then dragged to River Wylye
- Exeter
- N
- 0 — 50 miles
- 0 — 80 km

The Bluestone Route

1 Stones dragged from the Preseli Mountains to Milford Haven.

2 Loaded onto barges or rafts and sailed along the coast of Wales and across to Avonmouth.

3 Floated up the Rivers Avon and Frome, then unloaded at Frome in Somerset.

4 Dragged about 10 kilometres to the River Wylye, then loaded onto barges and floated downstream to the river Avon.

5 River Avon carries stones to within about 3 kilometres of Stonehenge, where they are unloaded and dragged the rest of the way.

how could these enormous stones have been brought over 350 kilometres, from Wales to Salisbury Plain, without any kind of machinery to help?

Transporting the stones needed a combination of manpower and cleverness. The bluestones were cut roughly to shape in the quarry, then hundreds of men dragged them on rollers or sledges to the port of Milford Haven. They were loaded onto barges or rafts and sailed to England. Using a combination of dragging and water travel, the bluestones finally made their way to Stonehenge.

Circle designers

After the Second World War, a retired professor of engineering, called Alex Thom, took his tools and began to make accurate scientific measurements of stone circles. No one had ever done this before, and what Thom found seemed incredible. His discoveries caused historians to review their ideas of what the **megalithic** world had been like, and pointed the way to finally solving the riddle of what stone circles were for.

Geometry of the circles

Thom found that almost all the stone circles had been built using precise mathematical knowledge. The ancient circle builders had understood **geometry** very well. Often they had used mathematical techniques that were not thought to have been discovered until much later. One example of this was the **Pythagorean triangle**, a triangle in which one corner is a right angle. Pythagoras, the Greek mathematician who is credited with inventing the formula for this type of triangle, lived from about 560 BC to 480 BC. But stone circle designers were using Pythagorean triangles thousands of years before this.

Pythagoras, the Greek mathematician, put into theory what stone circle builders had put into practice.

People sometimes claim that the stones must have been put up by primitive people, because some of the 'circles' are not properly circular. Thom's survey of the circles showed that in fact the non-circular sites had been designed as either **ellipses** or elongated (stretched) circles. Both of these shapes are more complicated to design than plain circles.

The megalithic yard

Thom's most amazing discovery was that many megalithic circles had been built using a standard unit of measurement, which he called a 'megalithic yard'. This megalithic yard had been used by hundreds of circle designers, building circles thousands of kilometres apart, and over a period of thousands of years. Historians had previously thought that different megalithic tribes did not share measurements. Thom's incredible findings seemed to prove this wrong.

Making a Pythagorean triangle

Megalithic circle designers worked on the ground, and this is the best place for you to copy them. All you need is three tent pegs and a length of cord with thirteen knots tied in it. The knots need to be exactly the same distance apart.

1 *Put a peg through the first and last knots, and into the ground.*
2 *Put another peg through the fourth knot and into the ground, keeping the rope tight between the pegs.*
3 *Now put the third peg through the eighth knot and stretch the rope tight on both sides, then push the peg into the ground.*

*Congratulations: you have made a megalithic Pythagorean triangle! The **ratio** of the sides is 3:4:5.*

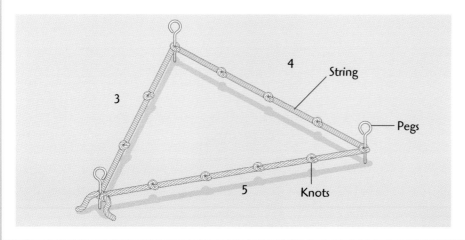

Calendars in stone

Once scientists began to understand that the stone circles were more complicated and far more carefully designed than they had thought, they began to think about them in a different way. They also began to look more carefully at the similarities between the circles. Why did so many of them share particular features?

Midsummer and midwinter

Many circles contain stones marking the position of the sun on **Midsummer** or **Midwinter** Day. These dates would also have been crucial to megalithic people. On Midwinter Day, for example, they would know that from then on the days were going to get longer. In practical terms, this meant that they would be able to work out whether they had enough food left to last the rest of the winter. But megalithic people would also have celebrated the fact that each year was like the last: winter was not going to continue forever, it was going to end, just as it had the year before.

The sun rises behind a stone circle. As the seasons change, so does the position of the sunrise and sunset in relation to the stones.

Predicting the seasons

Stonehenge and Avebury, for example, both feature arcs of nineteen stones. These stones are placed so that each one marks off how much the sun has moved its position in the sky after one year. At the end of nineteen years, the sun has returned to its original position in the sky. This does not seem particularly important to us now, but to **megalithic** people it would have been a different matter. Their lives depended on the seasons and the years changing in a way that they could predict. Without knowing this, they would not have been sure when to plant crops, when winter was about to arrive, or when spring was due to bring warmer weather.

*Sunset at Callanish, a circle with a stone that **aligns** with the Sun on Midsummer's Day.*

Computer modelling

Each year the Earth changes its position a little in relation to the Sun, Moon and stars. This means that they appear in a slightly different place in the sky from one year to the next. This difference is tiny, but over thousands of years it builds up to make a noticeable difference. The stone circles were built between 3000 and 5000 years ago, so scientists have to use computers to work out where the Sun, Moon and stars would have appeared in the night sky at that time.

Megalithic mysteries

Using computers and modern measuring techniques, scientists have been able to provide answers to some of the questions that surround ancient stone circles. We now know how the giant stones were moved to the site of the circle, how they were raised into position and that they were used as a kind of calendar. But there are other mysteries waiting to be solved. Perhaps the greatest mystery of all relates to the position of ancient sites when viewed on a map. Strange **alignments** can sometimes be seen.

Triangles on the landscape

In the west of England, the stone circle at Stonehenge and two other **megalithic** sites, Grovely Castle and the old settlement at Old Sarum, make up the three corners of a triangle with exactly equal sides, each measuring 9 kilometres. If the lines that make up the sides of the triangle are continued, they each lead straight to other ancient sites.

Another, even larger triangle exists – its three corners are Stonehenge, Lundy Island off the coast of Devon, and the site at Preseli from which Stonehenge's bluestones were **quarried**. The ancient name for Lundy is *Ynys Elen*, which means 'island of the elbow' or 'island of the angle'.

Ley lines

Ley lines were discovered – though some people say they were invented – by a man named Alfred Watkins. In 1925, he published a book called *The Old Straight Track*, in which he claimed that the ancient sites in his local area were all connected by straight lines. He called these lines 'leys'. The sites included ancient churches (which had often been built on even older sites), castles, **standing stones**, hilltop forts, gates, crossroads and stone circles. Watkins' definition of a ley line was that it was a straight line on which five sites of this kind were found within five kilometres.

Almost all stone circles are situated on ley lines. If someone can one day explain what ley lines are and how they work, it may help us to understand more about the circles. But many scientists do not accept that ley lines exist, so it could be many years before this particular mystery is solved – if it ever is!

Dowsing for ley lines

Dowsing is a mysterious art dating from long ago. It involves using two sticks to search for underground water, as a way of finding a place to dig a well. The sticks are held lightly, one in each hand. As the dowser walks over water the sticks come together. Some people think that it is also possible to dowse for ley lines. They argue that ley lines are channels of energy under the earth, which a skilled dowser can detect. There is little evidence for this theory.

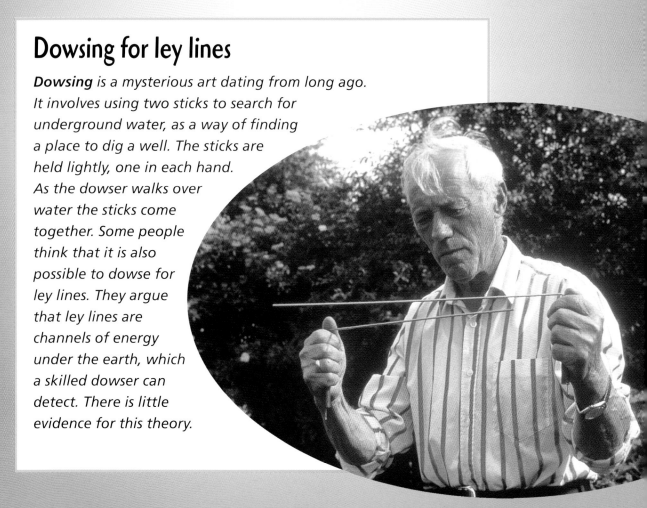

Decide for yourself

The mysteries of the stone circles have baffled people for many thousands of years. Before modern science, people could not imagine how the circles could have been built. They gave them supernatural characteristics as a result, saying they had been made by the Devil, or witches, or wizards.

Today, very few people are willing to accept explanations like these. We are used to being able to understand how things work, and generally carry on investigating until we find an explanation that is satisfactory. Then that explanation has to be tested through experiments. This is the basis of modern science: having an idea and testing it to see if it works.

What has science shown us?

This scientific approach has offered us some insights into why the stone circles were built and what they might have been used for:

- Science has shown how **megalithic** people moved giant stones over huge distances, using a combination of dragging the stones and floating them on barges. Also, we know how these giant stones were put into place.
- Using **carbon dating**, scientists were able to discover the true age of stone circles, which turned out to be far older than anyone had previously guessed. Many of the stones dated from 5000 years ago, or about 3000 BC.
- Using modern surveying equipment, Alexander Thom was able to make the first proper plans of stone circles. This led Thom to suggest that the stones were laid out in a deliberate pattern, and that their position meant they could be used as an enormous calendar.

- Scientists have since been able to use computers to work out what the night sky looked like when the circles were built. We now know that many circles **align** with the movements of the Sun and Moon.

Some mysteries remain

Some mysteries still remain unsolved. We don't yet really know what happened at the circles – were they the site of human **sacrifices**, or did the bones that have been found there come from some other source? Were they used for festivals, or for religious ceremonies? Most of all, how is it that circles and other ancient sites seem to be positioned along straight lines?

Science has not yet found a way to unravel these mysteries. But the age of the circles was a mystery until the invention of carbon dating, so perhaps in a few years scientists will be able to answer other questions about the circles. Then again, perhaps the secrets of the stone circles died out with the megalithic people, and no one will ever know the true answers.

Long Meg and her Daughters, a stone circle in Cumbria, UK. Why do you think it was built?

Glossary

align arrange in a straight line

alignment group of things that are arranged in a straight line

barrow ancient grave mound, often called a tumulus. The countryside of northern and western Europe contains many barrows, which are thousands of years old.

burial chamber room in which the body of someone who has died is kept. Burial chambers are usually either underground or partly underground.

cairn mound of stones that is used as a monument or landmark of some kind

carbon dating scientific method for discovering how old something is by measuring the amount of a particular element it contains

computer model three-dimensional model of an object or place that is created on a computer. Computer models can be viewed from different angles and allow scientists and engineers to test their ideas without having to build expensive models in real life.

cursed associated with evil in some way, or destined to come to harm. Many stone circles had a reputation as evil places, but usually this was because of rumours started by Christian priests in the Middle Ages.

dolmen ancient tomb with a large, flat stone laid on top of upright ones

dowsing method of finding where water runs underground. Dowsing is an ancient art, which scientists do not yet understand.

druids leaders of a nature-loving religion which existed in the British Isles before the time of the Roman invasion. Druidism was quickly destroyed by Christianity.

element chemical that cannot be broken down into the different parts that make it up. Iron, gold and potassium are all elements.

ellipse regular oval shape

embankment raised line of earth or stone, often used to carry a path or road, or to enclose a space

geometry branch of mathematics that is concerned with shapes and lines

gory to do with blood and guts

lintel horizontal piece of wood or stone that supports the top of a door

megalithic from the time of the stone circle builders. The name comes from the Latin words *mega* (big) and *lithos* (stone).

menhir single standing stone

midsummer middle of summer. Midsummer Day falls around 21 June and is the day on which it is light for the longest time.

midwinter middle of winter. Midwinter Day falls around 21 December and is the day on which it is light for the shortest time.

Pythagorean triangle triangle in which one of the corners is a right angle

quarried cut out of the ground. Minerals and rocks, such as coal and iron, are quarried.

quoits flat, circular stones that are part of a dolmen. Their name comes from the game of quoits, in which a heavy, flat, iron ring is thrown at an iron peg.

ratio mathematical way of showing how one number relates to another. For example, 3:4 has the same ratio as 600:800, it is a result of the original number being multiplied by 20.

sabbath weekly religious day of rest. Some religious people think that it is wrong to play music or dance on the sabbath day.

sacrifice killing an animal or person as an offering to a god

sarsen kind of sandstone that was used by stone circle builders at Stonehenge and Avebury

shroud piece of cloth used to cover a dead body

standing stone long stone that has been stood up on end, so that it is much taller than it is wide

trilithon group of three stones, two standing upright and the third lying across the top of the gap between them

Index

Titles in the *Can Science Solve* series include:

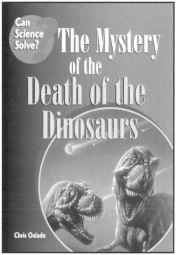

Hardback   0 431 01623 2

Hardback   0 431 02040 X

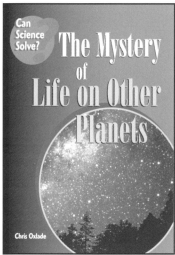

Hardback   0 431 01624 0

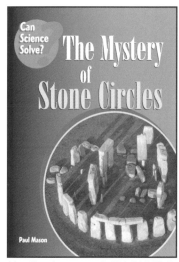

Hardback   0 431 01625 9

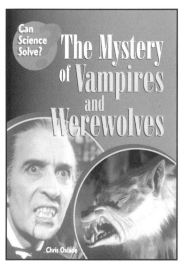

Hardback   0 431 01622 4

Find out about the other titles in this series on our website www.heinemann.co.uk/library